UFOS

BY NADIA HIGGINS

EPIC

BELLWETHER MEDIA · MINNEAPOLIS, MN

EPIC BOOKS are no ordinary books. They burst with intense action, high-speed heroics, and shadows of the unknown. Are you ready for an Epic adventure?

This edition first published in 2014 by Bellwether Media, Inc.

No part of this publication may be reproduced in whole or in part without written permission of the publisher. For information regarding permission, write to Bellwether Media, Inc., Attention: Permissions Department, 5357 Penn Avenue South, Minneapolis, MN 55419.

Library of Congress Cataloging-in-Publication Data

Higgins, Nadia, author.
  UFOs / by Nadia Higgins.
     pages cm. – (Epic. Unexplained Mysteries)
  Summary: "Engaging images accompany information about UFOs. The combination of high-interest subject matter and light text is intended for students in grades 2 through 7"– Provided by publisher.
  Audience: Ages 7-12.
  Includes bibliographical references and index.
  ISBN 978-1-62617-107-7 (hardcover : alk. paper)
  1. Unidentified flying objects–Juvenile literature. 2. Curiosities and wonders–Juvenile literature. I. Title.
  TL789.2.H54 2014
  001.942–dc23
                          2013041426

Designed by Jon Eppard.

Printed in the United States of America, North Mankato, MN.

TABLE OF CONTENTS

WHAT WAS THAT?

A loud buzzing sound wakes up a quiet neighborhood. People gather outside to see what is going on. Suddenly, a green light shines in the sky.

At first they think it is a plane. But they notice it is not moving. What could be **hovering** in the sky? The light disappears before they have an answer.

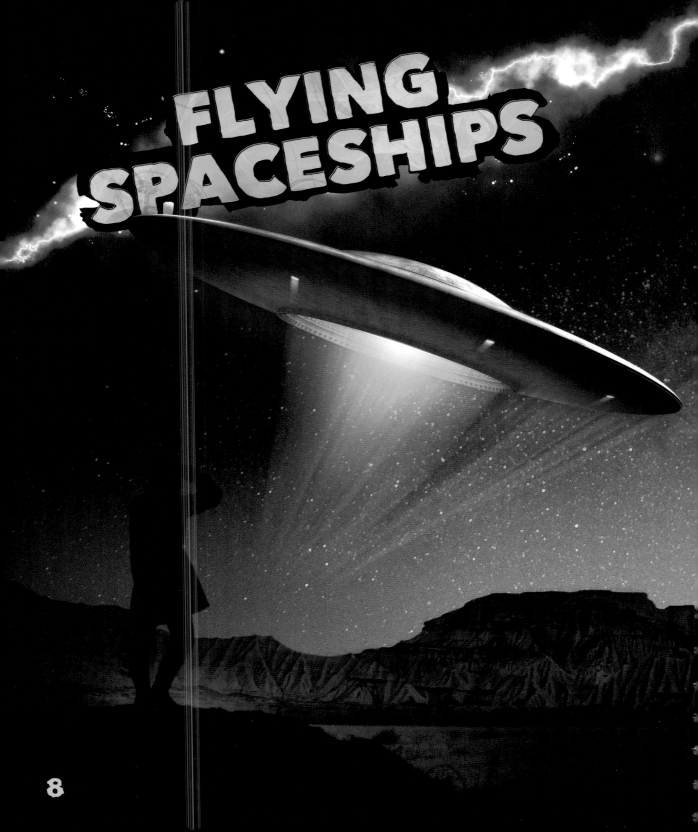

FLYING SPACESHIPS

Every year, thousands of people report seeing UFOs. These are **unidentified** flying objects. Many people believe UFOs are **alien** spaceships.

IS ANYONE OUT THERE?

Many scientists believe there are billions of other planets that might support life.

In 1947, a man found strange **debris** in a field in Roswell, New Mexico. The military **investigated**. First they said it was a **flying disc**. Then they changed their story.

ucer

Ramey Says Excitement Is Not Justified

General Ramey Says Disk Is Weather Balloon

Tehran, July 5, (P)—The flying saucer fever spread to Iran today.

Press reports from Zabool, Afghan frontier said residents there had observed strange "starlike bodies" in the sky which exploded loudly, leaving a cloud of smoke.

The newspaper Mehri Iran said the objects apparently had something to do with a secret weapon, which it dubbed "V-26."

Fort Worth, Texas, July 9 (P)— An examination by the army revealed last night that the mysterious objects found on a lonely New Mexico ranch was a harmless high-altitude weather balloon—not a grounded flying disk.

Excitement was high until Brig. Gen. Roger M. Ramey, commander of the Eighth air forces with headquarters here cleared up the mystery.

The bundle of unfoil broken wood beams and rubber remnants of a balloon were sent here yesterday by army air transport in the wake of reports that it was a flying disk.

But the general said the objects were the crushed remains of a ray wind target used to determine the direction and velocity of winds at high altitudes.

Warrant Officer Irving Newton forecaster at the army air force weather station here, said he saw them because they go much higher than the eye can see.

The weather balloon was found several days ago near the town of New Mexico by Rancher W. W. Brazel. He said he didn't think much about it until he saw Cyclone, N. M., last Saturday described the finding that he recovered the wreckage of a

FULL OF HOT AIR?
The Air Force soon claimed the flying disc was a weather balloon. This type of balloon is used to measure weather patterns.

11

Reports of UFO sightings increased after the Roswell crash. People also started to tell scary stories about aliens. Some claimed they had been **abducted**!

NO ANSWERS

From 1952 to 1969, the Air Force looked into more than 12,000 UFO reports. Around 700 of these are still unsolved.

13

TRUE OR FALSE?

McMinnville, Oregon
1950

Hangzhou, China
2010

Many people have taken pictures and videos of UFOs. Some people believe these are **evidence** of aliens.

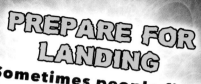

Sometimes people find strange patterns in fields. Many believe alien spaceships landed at these crop circles.

blimp

balloon

satellite

Skeptics do not believe aliens visit Earth. They think stories about aliens are made up. They argue that UFOs are **blimps**, balloons, or **satellites**.

VENUS ➡

NIGHTLIGHT

Venus is often mistaken for a UFO. The bright planet sometimes shines like a light.

Others think the military
invented UFOs. They believe
UFO stories cover up tests on
secret technology.

FAMOUS UFO SIGHTINGS

Near Mount Rainier, Washington (1947)
Pilot Kenneth Arnold sees nine disc-shaped objects zip by his plane.

Roswell, New Mexico (1947)
A rancher finds strange pieces of shiny material in a field.

Lubbock, Texas (1951)
For two months, strange lights zip across the sky in a curved pattern.

On U.S. Route 3 in New Hampshire (1961)
Betty and Barney Hill see a strange light in the sky while driving. They claim aliens came in a flying disc and abducted them.

Belleville, Wisconsin (1987)
Tube-shaped objects fly out of forests in the daytime.

Gulf Breeze, Florida (1987-1990)
Edward Walters says he is often visited by aliens. He claims to have photos of UFOs to prove it. Hundreds of others in the area also report UFOs.

Are aliens visiting our planet in UFOs? Or are people getting carried away with their imaginations? The answer remains up in the air.

GLOSSARY

abducted—captured against one's will

alien—a being from another planet

blimps—floating aircraft that do not have wings

debris—pieces left over from something that has been destroyed

evidence—physical proof of something

flying disc—an alien spaceship that is shaped like a pie plate; flying discs are also called flying saucers.

hovering—staying in one place in the air

investigated—searched for clues to find out the facts about something

satellites—objects in space that orbit Earth

skeptics—people who doubt the truth of something

unidentified—unknown

TO LEARN MORE

At the Library

Halls, Kelly Milner. *Alien Investigation: Searching for the Truth about UFOs and Aliens*. Minneapolis, Minn.: Millbrook Press, 2012.

Perish, Patrick. *Are UFOs Real?* Mankato, Minn.: Amicus, 2014.

Portman, Michael. *Are UFOs Real?* New York, N.Y.: Gareth Stevens Publishing, 2013.

On the Web

Learning more about UFOs is as easy as 1, 2, 3.

1. Go to www.factsurfer.com.

2. Enter "UFOs" into the search box.

3. Click the "Surf" button and you will see a list of related Web sites.

With factsurfer.com, finding more information is just a click away.

INDEX

The images in this book are reproduced through the courtesy of: oorka/ inigo cia, front cover (composite), pp. 8-9; Alexey Stiop/ jehsomwang, pp. 4-5 (composite); John Panella/ TijanaM/ 21, pp. 6-7 (composite); M L Pearson/ Alamy, p. 10; Mary Evans/ Photo Researchers, Inc./ Science Source, p. 11; jehsomwang/ Dudarev Mikhail/ RCL, pp. 12-13 (composite); Science Source, p. 14 (top); Europics/ Newscom, p. 14 (bottom); Solent News/ Splash News/ Newscom, p. 15; ER_09, p. 16 (top); NASA, p. 16 (middle); Mechanik, p. 16 (bottom); Stocktrek Images/ SuperStock, pp. 16-17; Fer Gregory/ Department of Defense, pp. 18-19 (composite); Miguel A, p. 21.